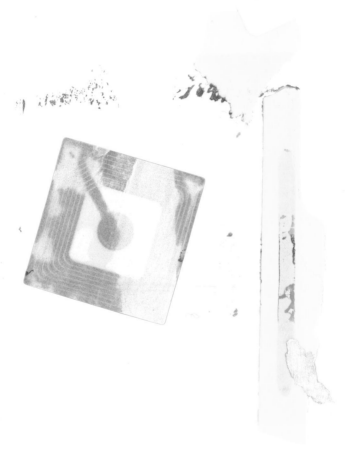

ANIMAL
RIGHTS

WILD ANIMAL
REHABILITATION

Jessie Alkire

**Checkerboard
Library**

An Imprint of Abdo Publishing
abdopublishing.com

abdopublishing.com

Published by Abdo Publishing, a division of ABDO, PO Box 398166, Minneapolis, Minnesota
55439. Copyright © 2018 by Abdo Consulting Group, Inc. International copyrights reserved in
all countries. No part of this book may be reproduced in any form without written permission
from the publisher. Checkerboard Library™ is a trademark and logo of Abdo Publishing.

Printed in the United States of America, North Mankato, Minnesota
102017
012018

THIS BOOK CONTAINS
RECYCLED MATERIALS

Design: Christa Schneider, Mighty Media, Inc.
Production: Mighty Media, Inc.
Editor: Megan Borgert-Spaniol
Cover Photographs: Shutterstock
Interior Photographs: Alamy, pp. 17, 19, 27; iStockphoto, p. 11; Shutterstock, pp. 4 (left, right), 5,
7, 8, 9, 13, 14, 15, 21, 23, 25, 28 (top, middle, bottom), 29 (left, middle, right)

Publisher's Cataloging-in-Publication Data
Names: Alkire, Jessie, author.
Title: Wild animal rehabilitation / by Jessie Alkire.
Description: Minneapolis, Minnesota : Abdo Publishing, 2018. | Series: Animal rights |
    Includes online resources and index.
Identifiers: LCCN 2017944028 | ISBN 9781532112621 (lib.bdg.) | ISBN 9781532150340 (ebook)
Subjects: LCSH: Wildlife rescue--Juvenile literature. | Wildlife rehabilitation--Juvenile
literature. | Animal rights movement--Juvenile literature. | Animal welfare--Juvenile literature.
Classification: DDC 639.96--dc23
LC record available at https://lccn.loc.gov/2017944028

CONTENTS

WHAT IS WILD ANIMAL REHABILITATION?

Have you ever come across a baby bird that had fallen from its nest? Or maybe you've discovered a deer that appeared to be injured. Animals large and small run into trouble every day. Humans often want to help. But most people are not equipped to care for a wild animal. This is a job for wild animal rehabilitators.

Rehabilitation, or rehab, is the process of bringing something back to a normal, healthy condition. Wild animal rehab is providing care to sick, injured, or orphaned wildlife. Rehabilitators know the proper way to transport and care for these animals. The rehabilitators also work with veterinarians to treat animal injuries and illnesses. Rehabilitated animals are not tamed or **domesticated**. Once the animals are healthy, they are returned to their natural **habitats**.

Wild animal rehabilitators can operate as individuals or organizations. Some focus on specific species, such as raptors and other birds. Others will take in any animals in need. They often help protect and preserve **endangered** species.

HUMANS & WILD ANIMALS

Wild animal rehab is largely a modern practice. Through much of history, it was more common for humans to **domesticate** or hunt wild animals. However, some groups did protect and care for wild animals.

In India, an ancient religion called Jainism established some of the first animal hospitals for wild and domestic animals. Jainism also banned eating animals and sacrificing them in religious ceremonies. Around 250 BCE, Emperor Ashoka ruled the Mauryan Empire in India. He banned the hunting of certain wild animals.

People in the United States began to show interest in caring for wild birds in the late 1800s. In 1896, the Massachusetts Audubon Society formed to protect the state's birds and their

Audubon societies around the world are named after American John James Audubon. He painted portraits of birds in the early 1800s.

habitats. Similar organizations were soon founded in other states. In 1903, the United States established its first National Wildlife Refuge. It protected the birds living on Florida's Pelican Island.

Increased interest in wildlife conservation led to the practice of rehabilitation. The first rehabilitators often worked out of their own homes. Soon, organizations and institutions began rehabilitating wild animals too. Illinois's Trailside Museum of Natural History opened in 1932. It was one of the first formal animal rehab centers.

THE WILD ANIMAL MOVEMENT

Public interest in wildlife conservation increased throughout the 1960s and 1970s. People wanted to do more to protect wild animals and preserve their **habitats**. Nature centers, museums, and educational institutions became more involved in rehab efforts.

In the late 1960s and early 1970s, oil spills off the coast of California brought more attention to wildlife rehabilitation. These spills killed hundreds of seabirds and poisoned other marine life. Many people helped rehabilitate the birds affected by these oil spills. After a 1971 oil spill off the coast of San Francisco, more than 6,000 birds were taken in by rehab centers!

Rehabilitators use Dawn dishwashing liquid to clean oil off bird feathers.

The oil spills brought national attention to the importance of preserving wildlife. In 1972, the International Wildlife Rehabilitation Council (IWRC) was founded. This organization works to provide education on wild animal rehab. It does so through courses, an annual conference, and a published journal. The IWRC also has standards for the care and living conditions of wild animals in rehab. It has helped thousands of rehabilitators better care for sick, injured, and orphaned wildlife.

When coated in oil, feathers lose their ability to keep birds warm and dry. Oil also destroys feathers' air pockets that help birds float.

REHABILITATION CENTERS

Today, wild animal rehab centers take many different forms. Most rehabilitators work independently, caring for animals in their homes or in facilities they own. Organizations also employ professional rehabilitators. Some of these organizations are dedicated solely to rehabilitation. Others include zoos, nature centers, and educational institutions that have rehab programs.

Whether working independently or for an organization, all US wild animal rehabilitators must be licensed through their states. Each state has its own requirements for licensing. This often includes training at established rehab facilities and passing state-issued exams. Rehabilitators must also provide a certain standard of care and living conditions for wild animals.

After hatching, baby sea turtles are easy prey for crabs, birds, and other predators. Rehabilitators often take in weak or injured baby sea turtles so the animals have a better chance of survival.

Rehab centers need both indoor and outdoor cages or enclosures. Centers also require plenty of storage space for food, medicine, and supplies. Many facilities have vans or trucks for transporting animals.

Rehab centers can specialize in certain species or types of wild animals. For example, a facility may take in only orphaned infant animals or only bald eagles. But there are some organizations that rehabilitate many types of animals.

ADMITTING AN ANIMAL

Wild animal rehab facilities can vary greatly. But all rehabilitators care for animals with the goal of releasing them for survival in the wild. This begins with the collection of the sick, injured, or orphaned animals.

Rehabilitators are trained to capture and transport animals in a way that will keep both themselves and the animals safe. These workers have the proper clothing and tools to protect themselves from disease or injury. They also have appropriate equipment, cages, and **vehicles** for transporting the animals to rehabilitation facilities. Animal control officers, veterinarians, and other professionals are also often equipped to safely bring animals into rehab centers.

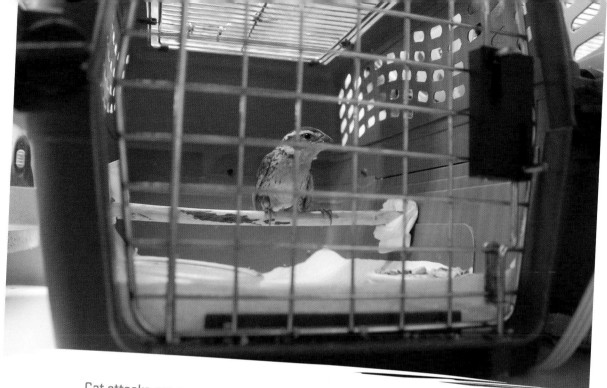

Cat attacks are a common cause of bird injury and death. Cat owners can help prevent these attacks by keeping their pets indoors.

Once an injured animal is admitted to a rehab center, workers determine the severity of its injuries. An animal with severe injuries is treated right away. If the animal is not severely injured, it is separated from humans for a short period. This helps calm the animal. Reducing an animal's **stress** greatly increases its chance of survival. The next step after admitting an animal is treatment and care.

WILD ANIMAL CARE

A thorough examination is the first step in treating an injured animal. Rehabilitators look for broken bones, wounds, and diseases. They also check for signs of **infection**, hunger, and **dehydration**.

Sometimes, veterinarians are needed to examine and treat animals. These doctors can provide the animals with medication, give **stitches**, insert feeding tubes, and more. With minor

treatments, animals may be released after 24 hours of observation. But most animals are kept at rehab centers for further care.

Animals admitted to rehab typically receive constant care and observation. This is called critical care. Critical care can last a few days to a few months.

RIGHTS
SPOTLIGHT

TOOLA THE SEA OTTER

Toola the sea otter was rescued by a California aquarium in 2001. She was sick at the time, and pregnant too. Toola's baby didn't survive. But another sea otter pup was rescued at the same time. The aquarium staff introduced the pup to Toola. Toola took care of him like he was her own. The pup was later released into the Pacific Ocean.

Female animals that care for orphaned infant animals are called surrogate mothers.

Toola proved that **captive** otters can help successfully rehabilitate wild otter pups. She went on to raise 12 more otter pups. Eleven of them were released back into the wild!

Orphaned infant animals often need the most critical care. Baby squirrels, for example, are kept in **incubators** to control their body temperature. Rehabilitators must also feed these infant animals every few hours. Certain infant birds require feeding multiple times each hour!

Severely injured animals often need as much critical care as infant animals. Animals with severe injuries may have strict medication schedules. Some injuries prevent these animals from feeding themselves. Workers must provide constant care to the animals to keep them fed and watered. Rehabilitators also observe these animals closely for signs of **infection** or other medical problems.

Once animals no longer need critical care, their care schedules become more relaxed. However, the animals are still closely watched. They are fed highly specialized diets. The wild animals are also kept in quiet, calm surroundings to reduce **stress**.

A final step in rehab is reintroducing an animal to members of its species. This encourages interaction. The rehabilitated animal can also learn necessary survival skills by observing its own species.

Many wild animal rehab centers rely on volunteers to help feed animals, clean cages, and more.

RETURN TO THE WILD

When an animal is healthy or grown enough to return to the wild, it is prepared for release. The animal is usually moved to an outdoor enclosure. This helps it get used to the **habitat** it will be released in. An outdoor enclosure also gives the animal more room to strengthen its muscles and express its natural behaviors. For example, eagles are first released in large flight chambers. This allows them to stretch their wings and fly before release into the wild.

The timing of an animal's release is important. Release should occur in mild weather. Extreme temperatures or conditions make it difficult for an animal to adjust to the wild. The animal should also be released in a season when its food source is abundant.

Once the season and weather are appropriate, the animal is taken to a release location. For an adult animal, this location is near where the animal was found. The animal can then join its family or territory. An orphaned animal is taken to a location that gives the animal its best chance of survival. This is a location where the animal will have access to food, water, nests or dens, and mates.

Marine mammals are often rescued from public beaches and other areas unfit for wildlife. Rehabilitators usually release the animals in different locations that are still within the animals' ranges.

REHAB CONCERNS

Unfortunately, not all animals can be released back into the wild. In some cases, it is because the animals became dependent on humans. They can no longer survive in the wild. Cases like these raise a common criticism of wild animal rehab. In rescuing an animal, rehabilitators can make it unfit for release.

Another criticism of wild animal rehabilitation is cost. It can cost thousands of dollars to care for just one animal. Critics argue this is a waste of money when the animal cannot return to the wild. Even successful rehab only affects individual animals, not entire species. Many critics feel this money is better spent on **habitat** preservation and other conservation efforts.

However, the main argument against rehab is that it is unnatural. Many experts believe wild animals should be left alone. Ecosystems rely on weak, sick, and injured animals to provide food for predators. Rehab interferes with this natural process.

Fawns sometimes appear to be orphaned when they are not. Deer commonly leave their fawns alone for several hours at a time.

Many wildlife professionals discourage rehab if animal distress is caused by natural forces. They also warn that infant animals that appear to be abandoned are not necessarily orphaned. These professionals often argue it is best to leave wild animals alone. But many rehabilitators believe that no animal should have to suffer. They attempt to save every individual life they can.

CALL OF THE WILD

Critics may believe rehabilitating wild animals goes against nature. But **advocates** argue that most animals in rehab centers are there because of human interference with nature, not because of natural causes. Chemicals, plastic waste, and other pollutants of human activity kill thousands of animals each year. Wild animals are also hit by cars, injured by hunters, and caught in traps.

Because humans cause so much harm to wildlife, rehabilitators believe it is our responsibility to help animals in need. They believe we should treat wild animals with respect. Rehabilitators care for suffering animals to give them a second chance at life and freedom.

Rehabilitators also believe the work they do benefits humans. In working closely with wild animals, rehabilitators learn about many types of wildlife. They can then educate others about these animals and how to reduce human **impact** on wildlife.

Rabies is a type of disease that animals can pass to humans. Raccoons, foxes, skunks, and bats are common carriers of rabies.

Rehabilitators also learn and share with others the ways wild animals can **impact** humans. Wild animals often carry diseases that can be passed to humans. Rehabilitators treat these animals so they cannot **infect** other animals and humans. Rehab centers may also research and track diseases in certain species. They can notify the public and government agencies of disease outbreaks. In this way, wild animal rehab makes the world safer for both animals and humans.

FINDING AN INJURED ANIMAL

The care rehabilitated animals receive is highly specialized. Only a licensed rehabilitator can provide this service. But the public can help too! The best way to do this is to watch out for wild animals that need help.

To determine if an animal needs help, look for signs of distress. These signs include bleeding, shivering, and crying. Look for broken limbs or missing fur or feathers. If you see an infant animal on its own, search for a dead parent nearby. But remember, a lone infant animal is not necessarily an orphan. It may simply be on its own while the parent finds food.

No matter the situation, the decision to help a wild animal should be left to professionals. If you see an animal in distress, call a wild animal rehab center near you. A worker will usually come to safely capture and transport the animal. If there are no centers near you, contact an animal shelter, animal control center, or veterinarian.

While waiting for help, keep your distance. Never handle, touch, or try to feed an animal in the wild. Even small animals can injure you. And many animals carry diseases that harm humans. Once the animal is taken, you can contact the rehab center for updates!

Infant squirrels sometimes fall out of their nests. Their mothers usually rescue them within a few hours. If this does not happen, the squirrel is likely orphaned.

FUTURE OF REHABILITATION

Human activity continues to affect wildlife. In 2010, the United States experienced the largest marine oil spill in history. For more than 80 days, oil leaked into the Gulf of Mexico. The **disaster** killed thousands of birds, sea turtles, and other wildlife.

Chemicals, plastic, and other pollutants are a constant threat to wild animals and their **habitats**. Experts argue that the best way to help these animals is by reducing human **impact**. By focusing efforts on protecting wildlife, there will be less need for rehab.

There are many ways that humans can do this on an individual level. Picking up loose trash around bodies of water helps prevent water pollution that affects marine wildlife. Volunteering or **donating** to wildlife conservation efforts is another way to help.

Brown pelicans were greatly affected by the 2010 US oil spill. Rehabilitated birds were released off Florida's eastern coast.

Scientists, conservationists, and rehabilitators don't always agree about wild animal rehab. However, the public is increasingly interested in wild animal welfare. Demand for wild animal rehab will likely continue to grow. Meanwhile, rehabilitators research better diets, medicines, and living conditions for their animal patients. They continue to improve their methods of caring for animals and releasing them back to their wild homes!

TIMELINE

250 BCE Emperor Ashoka rules the Mauryan Empire in India. He bans the hunting of certain wild animals.

1896 The Massachusetts Audubon Society is founded. Similar organizations soon follow.

1903 The first US National Wildlife Refuge is established to protect the birds living on Florida's Pelican Island.

1932 The Trailside Museum of Natural History opens in River Forest, Illinois. It soon begins rehabilitating wild animals.

1971 More than 6,000 birds are taken in by rehab centers after a San Francisco oil spill.

1972 The IWRC is founded.

2001 Toola the sea otter is rescued by a California aquarium. She helps raise and rehabilitate otter pups.

2010 The largest marine oil spill in history occurs in the Gulf of Mexico.

BECOME AN ANIMAL ADVOCATE

Do you want to become an advocate for wild animal rehabilitation? Here are some steps you can take today!

Spread the word. Education is key! Tell your family and friends all about wild animal rehabilitation.

Donate. Many rehab centers rely on donations. You can donate money, food, or other supplies!

Reduce your impact. Try not to harm animals through your everyday activities. Avoid leaving trash and food outdoors, and watch for animals when riding in the car.

Be watchful. Watch for injured or orphaned animals outside. Contact a rehabilitation center near you if you find an animal that needs help.

GLOSSARY

advocate – a person who defends or supports a cause.

captive – held or kept. Captive animals are wild animals kept and cared for by humans.

dehydration – loss or removal of water. When lost or used water is not replaced, an animal becomes dehydrated.

disaster – an event that causes damage, destruction, and often loss of life.

domesticate – to adapt something to life with humans. A domestic animal has been domesticated.

donate – to give. A donation is something that is given.

endangered – in danger of becoming extinct.

habitat – a place where a living thing is naturally found.

impact – a strong effect.

incubator – a chamber in which temperature and other conditions are controlled. Incubators are often used to protect newborn babies or infant animals.

infection – an unhealthy condition caused by something harmful, such as bacteria. To infect is to pass on an infection.

stitches – special threads that are used to close a wound.

stress – strain or pressure.

vehicle – something used to carry or transport. Cars, trucks, airplanes, and boats are vehicles.

ONLINE RESOURCES

Booklinks
NONFICTION
NETWORK
FREE! ONLINE NONFICTION RESOURCES

To learn more about wild animal rehabilitation, visit **abdobooklinks.com**. These links are routinely monitored and updated to provide the most current information available.

INDEX